On Tact, & the Made Up World

 Kuhl House Poets
edited by Mark Levine and Ben Doller

On Tact, & the Made Up World

MICHELE GLAZER

University of Iowa Press

Iowa City

University of Iowa Press, Iowa City 52242
Copyright © 2010 by Michele Glazer
www.uiowapress.org
Printed in the United States of America

Design by Sara T. Sauers

The University of Iowa Press is a member of Green Press Initiative and is committed to preserving natural resources.

Printed on acid-free paper

LCCN: 2010922739
ISBN-13: 978-1-58729-908-7
ISBN-10: 1-58729-908-9

for John

Contents

THREE

Acknowledgments

I thank the editors of these journals, in which some of these poems first appeared: *American Letters and Commentary*: "Green Animals"; *Black Warrior Review*: "The least amount of stirred air a figure needed"; *Boston Review*: "Metonymic Sonnet," "What so ever you"; *Burnside Review*: "To the rückenfigur"; *Cranky*: "Two Descending a Staircase"; *Crazyhorse*: "That Would be Whidbey," "bright things," "Trace"; *Denver Quarterly*: "In the lava tube," "The least part best"; *Field*: "Part of which is remembered and the other part is not forgotten"; *Greatcoat*: "manifesto"; *Gulf Coast*: "To the better view"; *Iowa Review*: "Child and Woman," "Distances at Sea"; *Lo-Ball*: "Notes on Tact & the Made Up World"; *New Orleans Review*: "Say the Unseen", "Fungus, with Daguerreotype"; *Packingtown Review*: "The rabbi is pressed into service"; *Pleiades*: "Mattress"; *Ploughshares*: "Worm, (to a rumor of lilies)"; *Poetry Daily* (reprint): "Green Animals"; *Willow Springs*: "All the holes in the bird blind say" (retitled "Every hole in the bird blind says"), "I didn't think much about what it was."

Thanks to the Oregon Arts Commission for its financial support, and the boost in spirits that came with it.

I am deeply grateful to Mark Levine.

To Mary Szybist, Ursula Irwin, and Tracy Dillon—my gratitude and affection.

ONE

I didn't think much about what it was

Something about the evening causes the walkers-by to walk awkwardly so that the one watching
watches to see if they might grow more graceful—

Is it the wet cold earth? Or something in the child's foot as if sideways was the straightest way?

The music is background to the children. To the girl in pink moving lap to lap to lap, lifted,
snuggled, patted, slapped gently. When you die you exempt yourself, you take your
self with you out of the trouble the world's in. There was always a face that loved that child.

About her, these, now, in their lives: small girl, old woman, teenager in a tight shirt; "Barbie,"
her chest says and there's a general stumbling up the tortured grass to the orchestral
War of 1812. Because it's dark. Because we're brief. A bat flies over head, squeaking and
tangled in no one's hair. As if it had consequences. Shortly even so the bridge lights up.

Trace

Out of the drainage ditch
and something

of how the reed
reaches makes the rag

of childhood twist,
the piled-up voices

rising reaffirm
the ditch.

. . .

ditch:
the flows meet here
and blown seeds from the road's
eithersides and field margins,
the undigestables birds passing drop
and trash passersby
flip out of their rushing side-windows.
A wilderness of small animal
carcasses moves under the water.
Murk and dross in-
habit the surface. Debris sinks.
The surface inhibits reflection while floating oil reflects
obsolete iridescences and the ditch—

the ditch in all its mergings and musings
presents itself—
an incongruous estuary.

. . .

You're sped past all this.
Your father is driving.
Your mother's asleep in the front seat.

. . .

Past cattails ditch-ridden
to the place imagined
is the place felt—

the fraught blossom,
the naught and requisite
inkling
of something down there rattles you,

you are the only body
of water.

. . .

Your mother slept too much and at inappropriate times.
She'd nod off suddenly.
She didn't look at you enough.
She didn't see you when she looked.
Invisible became a way of being right.

. . .

Trace is the scar
itself and the finger tip moving
over the scar's lip.

. . .

Some bubbles escape from the gassy heart.

What's down there rises,
a fretwork of birds.
The cattails gave birth
in you to the feeling of loss
before loss happens.

Gave you thus:
the beginnings of a romantic imagination

. . .

and the reeds seen out of the passing window made
a passing landscape but you were the one moving and
where I want to go with this you went—

. . .

Debris seeks its natural angle of repose

as a word is uttered,

canted to topple,

as a word suffices,

might—oh

when woe won't.

Every hole in the bird blind says

match your shape to my shape
head to hole, your eye
to what I offer.
Sure enough, a duck

here, & over
there no sky, no duck.

One eye to a high hole
& the sky opens
to wires, & the arms
of high power transmission lines.

What little I know —
the formation they travel in,
the little they know of solitude
or progress.

Another hole lets in a pond
on which the light is failing. Ducks
paddle around, & coots
with their unlikely feet

churn water.
No two holes connect.
There are people
who believe that

we the people are the people
(finding among themselves
inevitable friendships & lovers
who are their destiny),

& find themselves
in one continuous scene.
I want to be that one
hole, low in the corner

admitting only
a few grasses.

If I remove all that is not
bird, I say,
the landscape will jump less;
he says *stain*

is what I let the landscape do to me.

In the lava tube

Fifty feet down the walls are wet. Scott
runs ahead trying the wet rocks out,
not looking back when his fingers drop
down a hole the light he carries.
On his legs the dark hairs repeat.

An adult hummingbird weighs as much as a copper penny

his father said. What stays with us?
What texture will fact have? His father left
and the boy fisted two hummingbirds,
crazed suns.
The precise weight of one thing
standing for another. Ape Cave is what

ever's left. Someone will enter it, someone
will make sense of what molten rock made
effortlessly.

Flüchtling

I crouched low at the hole where.
Prodded it with a stick where

something resembling sodden
feather, or fur, found
in the wild crab apple
the cavity———

       Lumpen, the body
       shifts. Loose parts in

       side, no more a nation.
       No borders there
       is a trembling.

       The everything-inside has lost
       its place,
       loose parts in slide,

       a nation of refugees.
       No knowing
       how to move

       because it is flesh disturbed.
       Because it has weight
       it will shift.

How shall the self remain,

                    how shall it self remain,

unheld?

But held yet in the mind

——————— and dragged inside.

Not where you found me but where you looked,

out of the switch grass
blood rushes
up
      ——flushed

Bird you say, (the mark on its tail)

Bird, and not where the mind suffers
its margins of attention,

here   I am   all but

(slim line of white,
                a mark on its tail)

Cup

The couple at the next table has just met so we surmise. I was going to say
so we surprise. The woman is in her late forties, blonde. Her date speaks
with an accent that isn't European. I sit nearer their table than John,
across from me, looking over my shoulder through the picture window at
traffic passing as the woman is explaining why she is cautious. Is telling
her date she wants a man she can trust. She is wondering why some people
oppose *social normalities* —— *accepting a behavior* —— I cannot hear into
their *personal lives*. When I ask John for his answer to the old question:
"what would you do with your life if you had six months, one year to live?"
he'll answer "get divorced" because he still has an idea of happiness.
He carries with him the spit-cup, the slick shocking foam from the infection
that lingers where the cancer is. *Extinction* is heard from the next table
is a drag. He is in love with Ann, another friend. We know what we don't see.
And I want to hear more,   I want to know more about that other life,
the one that's not personal.

Worm, (to a rumor of lilies)

Ach — the gravitas of the hunt.

I

Digestive turned blue so the woman said.

Said, *I write my own islands*, and red, red.

Was *urinary.*   Under the astigmatic lens
of her naked eye she followed the tracts.

Looking at worms for a long time she said
A worm in its lifetime moves short distances.

She knew to follow them.   How?

There is the solace of repetition.
I like to think she came to worms the way one

comes for the first time to love,
because sight fails.

II

Sight fails, love comes.
There was something I couldn't see.
Its systems are vivid the woman said

(I saw that), as I saw that

opened lengthwise it tended to curl,
closing its borders.
        She pinned it open.

Earth-Eater —

Secretor of Casings —

if the brain is wired for syntax
you are passion's syntax
made manifest,

and now my surface is changed and looked at.

III

Now that what is looked at is changed

what is looked for is gone, and even

an ancient worm in suspension

in its slender

test tube of formaldehyde carries

an air of something imagined.

And the woman

driven to dig for them,

they're out there

they smell like lilies.

IV

Name: Oregon Giant Earthworm (Driloleirus macelfreshi)
Status: Federal Candidate
Description: 2-foot long, pinkish-white earthworm
Overview: Oregon's giant earthworm was discovered in 1937, when a live specimen was unearthed in Salem
Distribution: Not much is known about these worms, and the extent of their distribution remains a mystery

What smelled like lilies after rain
curls back.

Everything is in there.

Directions to how it works.

What do you do for a shadow?
Dark earth—

how touch draws out

the something that doesn't gather up readily.

Untitled

I am not fond of it.

Its eyes have no interior looked at straight on in uncertain light.

It stops with two daily nor do I feed it more, nor does it fatten.

Nor does it waste.

I feel I should like it better.   Perhaps with affection it would grow on me.

Attachment is curious,

I should like to get under it.

I take it onto my lap, laying, first, a pillow there and my fingers on it.
This I call the passing of pleasure.

Only I feel the presence of something.
Human, a trespass.

On religion, war, nature, and the horse

John's unabstracted death for me.
Or to put it another way, the idea took possession of him.
These things happen.

A stone bench happened so I sat down on it.
Flowers nodded around
me with the requisite attention to spacing and abandon.
Now I seem to be, and to
know what it is to
disappear, to want to,

well,

my friendships seem a little
ragged today.
I should study nature instead.
The horse, for instance, the further away it runs
the more abstract.

Or the idea of the idyllic garden.
A child in a garden in Lebanon
whose legs and arms suddenly mismatch—
Alarmed by how they don't connect
burning flesh to burning flesh—
If I turn the page now how abstract is that.

TWO

That Would Be Whidbey

Would that be Whidbey over there?
Stare down at the water long enough
& the boat moves backwards.
                              Would there be

birds on a ferry?

There would be words,

yours?

This boat is not for sitting or sunning.
It is not for us to turn & dock anywhere.
I came for something.
Automobiles line up like the points
in the argument while all the time
were you thinking of pleasure?
Turn your engine off,

                    cormorant,
and that would be Whidbey.

Whidbey, if there are crows at the river.
Whidbey, where there are stumps.
There is only one way to get there:
departure.
                    But the river now
is jumpy in our wake,

                              & loneliness attends me
like the printed dress that keeps turning up one summer
on different women, (different colored hair).

Distances at Sea

for S. T.

I let my eyelids hover unshut like things adrift
in case a ship should pass at such distance I'd see it;
mine was a small boat.

My gunwales welcomed a wash
of the smaller fish casting themselves
sideways, flattening, clearing the sides

like high-jumpers in order
to take bites from my legs.
In that vastness they smelled my weakness.

How close the ships looked though
I couldn't make out a single person on board at that
——what *was* distance now

anyway?——only the dark
shape rising from the surface.
I thought they should see me.

In my body I felt as big.
I saw many ships, many days, and then the one
that, as I waved my handkerchief

faster, turned—
it grew larger.
The one who spotted me might

for a moment have looked up and then
beckoning his mate that a man in a flat boat
was — *over there*

look — readjusted his eye
to the scope. And he would go on
looking awhile

for a man among whitecaps riffling
like handkerchiefs until he was convinced
that he had made me up.

Mattress

ma^ttra^h, *place where something is thrown,*
mat, cushion, from ^tara^ha, *to throw;*
both from the Arabic.

I

John said it was a mattress tossed there
by an angry sea and I said or thrown
over the embankment from the highway
above by some sonofabitch and dragged
down there until we walked closer
and looking down from a fold of land
slightly above saw that it was a slab of
sandstone unlike the rest but similar and
beautiful now and then I said anyway,
anyway, I didn't believe in an angry sea.

II

                    The role of kiss is
to never swallow what it craves; not like
the heart, nothing breaks where it falls
though some one is left suspended until
another's mouth affixes. *I don't believe in—*
someone says and something ordinary
comes next, *god,* or *premarital sex.*
                    The earthworm, locking
its lips, takes in what it passes through. It
carves—   it craves— it filibusters
romance. I am troubled by belief: the
kiss repeats: see how it swallows and
where it lands and then the other body
bending so to catch it.

The rabbi is pressed into service

annually, on Ellen's birthdate, as every year
the day passes she would have turned 14, 15,
now 21, and we who are wrapped,

annually, in the gaze of the officiate
who in perfecting *sonorous* makes *monotonous*
the journey whereof he speaks, scatter, turn

our gazes to the patterned
wallpaper or that vase of carnations
and the drive-by rabbi

presses on, impressing
harder upon us, the assembled, the undifferentiated
living, the journey as he would

have us imagine it.
There is the *losing* and *finding*,
with assumptions of purpose

or ending at least
where there is a bed for the body
and a pillow to take

the impression your head leaves and briefly,
briefly keep it.
                    Rabbi

I am not wise, I
am not
lost.

      It is not her
journey anymore.

Won't you go home now
    Rabbi

lay your pressed
pants over the back of a chair,
and say a few words to your wife?

The least amount of stirred air a figure needed

She made floating islands—

didn't all islands float?
There were equivalencies of ocean
on both sides so we tried to imagine

what could be holding them up.
On the backs of what?
We were porous and watched her scoop
the burnished meringues out of the glass
dish while over there lit candles made the go-

round of pounded metal spin faster and
the figurines on top make a sound that was not
music but was like music, with the horns
in their hands and their mouths open.
How she could be that unhappy and not know it.

"I'll let you get that for me" is how my mother asked
for things she wanted so that what she wanted was no different
in her mind from what I wanted
to do for her and furthermore
because what she wanted

and what I wanted were the same
we were the same. Years before
I could parse her phrasings
I felt her claim.
"Do I like this?"

she asks now.
"Have I been here before?"
Now turn where, to
what? And how
does a candle burned low

make the go-round move.

Beds of Clandestine

1

Justin sleeps with a stuffed malaria parasite in his arms.

Walks on the bent-tops of his toes so it makes mine hurt.

Loses his arrow in a spring-leafed maple that hoarded the arrow that he wanted back.
Look for it he said to me when the leaves fall off.
Mine to find the half-hidden and I went back for it. I looked.

2

He breaks the pieces where they're scored—stacks them in his palm—places them on his tongue
rapidly one and one like laying tile before the glue dries.

The bars are full-sized and Justin is not but the favors he has scrounged are Hershey's 8 oz and now
they are Justin's, 7.

3

He was the larger twin, 3.8 pounds.
It was not one boy one day and the next another.

It's not my best advice to hide what you can't have in your back pocket
but pleasure spent and pleasure hoarded is more than twice itself.

To suck this hard it is like annexing the neighborhood.

4

Name everything that can break,

start with the obvious, the unintended, that buckles and holds
before it doesn't.

        Beds on either side of the chair upended
where the story ended and sleep wouldn't come.
Here smooth limbs insinuate. Something
blind undoes in darkness:

Child, this is a phase. Over the covers you flow.
Should wind be the mother
of fear, I feed you
Doubt. You toss caution to the floor.
Say *that's not scary* again, I'll show you.
Your pleasure's worn. You wear it —   the long alluvial grin.
If monster is all that scares you then I'll send them.
This is your childhood. Come in.

To the better view

With the better view out back,
we sit where storefronts dangle
starfish on strings (for your rearview mirror, for your Christmas tree),
shirts festooned with sandbuckets, and the titular rumble of ocean
is only a backdrop to a thought we might or might
not have, the way traffic sounds back home
(back home—the freeway sounds
around us—we tell ourselves *that's the ocean*).

There isn't much to do so we have to make do
and describe the early summer
visitors walking past licking their cones, the dogs their balls.
"Rat dog," John begins, loud enough they can hear but so what
is heard came out of which mouth? And George gives
"best of show" to a woman in white capris,
pink shades, cream-colored head
band "mostly for her purse" that is also white and who
would think to carry that to the beach?

The man sitting next to us
would hear our chatter if he weren't already somewhere
else. And wasn't it for him not us we said
all this?   Here's where
it gets rough. Where I should step off the porch and go inside
myself, move in closer, a little, to the scene
I've set myself
up to watch. Still there is an ocean inside
of the man sitting next to us.

In the ocean is a world of things
eating each other one of us
says and how is it
the show you're watching is not the show
you sit down for.
Now another passerby has stopped to admire the yellow Porsche
the man sitting next to us parked in front
of Osburns Ice Cream, then came up to sit on the porch and watch.

The least part best

There is the yellow missionstyletablelamp and the sack of white rocks
to lightup the front yard and if they aren't the things we like still there
is the feeling.

                        Thinking this felt like a new thought.
Like other people out there were accidents too. And there
is always a chance of finding something
and then they owe *you*.
We were busy too every one of us
formed in a sexual act and
bustedout with more or less instruction, we filled in our days.
But there was never a guarantee.
Or maybe it was the war and all that.   There was
the search for meaning and the ways we lived and the violet
shoes to match.

Say the Unseen

Say, the unseen needs a body in the world.
And that you are a woman to sit and watch would you
ask the icon be reduced to tears, to certainty?
I had been through the gift shop
crowded with nuns and pictures
of nuns but in the chapel where we sat
together in those drifted rows
and the icon alone was looked on —
                    Sybil of Discontent, why can't I
let disaster find its own way, why hurry it?
—— this waiting and wanting the weeping to start
and doubting it ——
proof to dissemble the face.
Waiting as I do for a certain word.
I have been through the gift shop, the walls
are crowded like the walls
of those rooms transfigured by the faces
of the dead and missing.
It is left to the experts to make the matches.
The country that practices torture has moved on.

What so ever you

When you are old and when you are removed from those people

who knew you back when and set down among strangers

you have no past. You are an old man

with his chin in his fists. You are an old man with his chin gracious when.

You are yet another old man

waiting in some line or other, gracious when

you let the woman in back of you go first because there is no hurry

whatsoever you are in.

It is not graciousness

that moves you

to the back of the line you look around you even now you see is growing.

You look around you at the young people like people you have never known

anyone like.   When you're young

you must be seen

by other people and for any reason

whatsoever.

Now you, the you you

must be seen by

glance in the mirror someone you would be

only if you were to stick around that long.

The people who knew you once——

what they saw when they saw you

was not the fish

pulled out of the water dangled

from the line it twists on.

Kids swoop down on their bright bicycles like flocks of birds ——

and run they run run red lights.

bright things

The old man who is dying   quietly, when he was two,

swallowed a safety pin.   who is almost still

now, then was a rambunctious child   putting a bright object into his mouth

because it was bright   because his mouth

was how he knew bright things —

there are the eitherends.   *then*

was decisive   declarative, and accidental.

the flesh ripped a little   you wouldn't think about that

in the moment   and the moment

tastes like something to be gotten rid of

fast, he coughs, tries   it sinks deeperin.

the mother would turn and everything

happens fast   the boy unable to speak   then, again

and the crazed woman descending on him.

THREE

Fungus, with Daguerreotype

*People usually think of a mushroom as a little creature, but most of the
action is underground.* —plant pathologist Dr. Thomas D. Bruns

—and wasn't it like us
to discover something
not hidden or lost
and liken it to other things.

Rhizomes mass in the shallow-
under — on top
toadstools poke out
scattershot, distant neighbors
but hardly a neighborhood.

Gorgeous Fungus.
Fungus of Repose,
of Urge, of Matter, not
penitent, not lost,

. . . a spreading map:
of spores, some trace of.

                    Whoever they are,
            the jewel box has for one
            hundred years kept them

face to face (the clasped hands,
the fragile color), the modest family
resemblance—

Lop off a node and no one's hurt—

Fungus, you disturb us—
who dispatches clonal shoots,
who kerns the basic unit
of biology; (for had we not imagined
ourselves one nation under. One?);

who makes one,
many,

under Michigan—under Washington—under ground   —they are not in any mind—they
have no discernible outline.

Left out in the light,
the bought-relatives—
irresistibly hinged and
tipped with color, and

glowing with the good health
of the immortals
who are looked at only
now

and no longer
looked after— pose
with that authentic formality
only the past offers—

the fugue stutters, the mind hitches——thickens resemblances— the imagination makes of them
a glowing consolation in
visible, under us.

aperture with wings

A child found it.   Hollie found it.

The bird had got its head caught

somehow between the rafter

and eave and hung there.

It was a sparrow someone guessed.

Somehow——

how many stories begin that way.

Or with some other small animal or other grubbing after

Your drawing of a horse

The smell of graphite brings back
the odor of animals
caught between the air and lead

in what they cannot stand apart from.

You drew the bones first to get the flesh on right,
leaving half the torso skeletal, the back half, falling
forward into flesh.

manifesto

robin in the birdbath below turns its head & with one lunge
manifests the smaller bird, perched like the last born on the cobble
edge, to fly off

then dips its breast into the solitary, shimmies water down its wings,
butters them thoroughly, both sides.

how so?

lifts one switching wing and turns its head back
to pick at whatsoever buried itself there

even in the beginning, perhaps because we are not
so young and have imparted our own space—

small part of what keeps me here, still   how your whole self weeping
once,
shook with

She would have to do what she could do with it

The caviar's pitched like a Midwest haystack but black.
It is the dean's house. The soup was delicious,

feint of lemon and scallops.
But the meat is incomprehensible

and swags off the plate on either side like the holiday
wreath on a white door, that red, and embellished with mint.

It is a fine cut from some part of the animal
but what? If she could keep it abstract:

it is a *lean cut*.   It is a *Featherbone, Rib Eye, Prime Rib, T-Bone*,
one of the above.

Remember the old tune? *She rode with the moon*
to her back and her back to the moon.

It is the dean's house. She contains herself.
He introduces her by the wrong name: *Melanie*, but close.

Green Animals

It may happen that we do not always want the most beautiful form, but one of our own designing. —Shirley Hibberd, quoted in *The Book of Topiary*, by Charles H. Curtis

MY TOPIARY IS A HEDGE AGAINST CONFUSION.

You have to come at it from a distance,
to walk up close to it to see the animal
is only from a distance:
then to be charmed by it.
The closer you get the more abstract.

     The dog is named for the variegated privet.
Walk away & the wind shakes it & the little leaves flicker,
perhaps, as if in happiness,
or, the water off.
It is not giving up anything nor is it
literal to a fault.

THE PRIVACY THE PRIVET PROMISED.

What had seemed headed in one direction took on *suddenly,*
a life of its own, the one thing forbidden.

The rule of time is you feel yourself growing older.

You see yourself from a distance that keeps getting longer.

THERE IS A FAILURE IN THE TOPIARY,

yet here we are, in the way the growing season
never lets the ragged ends of things be still.

Something will get us closer & then   Poof.
I think you see me for nearly what I am.

Metonymic Sonnet

To the chairman having his way in the chair with the minutes.

To the motion he makes to suspend them.

To a hole in the sky

wide enough to see through.

Let's sew this up, says the chairman.

To the matter at hand

and the handle he has on it. To the hand he has in it.

And to the secretary, writing it down, *taking the minutes*.

The chair sits.

His face flushes like a sun gathering color before the sky's won over and the dark takes hold.

Then moistens. The chair loosens his tie.

To the consummate still life:

the conference table and the water glasses sweating

and the coat tossed over the back of the chair.

To the rückenfigur

to describe a viewpoint that includes another person seen from behind
viewing a scene spread out before the viewer: rückenfigur

Too
tired to turn

contentment
fills them.

The pockets
in their backs

&
necks & butts small

rocks fill in,
soak

up the last.
What turns

then, what lingers?
What scent,

whose shoulders thus
placed direct

our gaze
—there

to mean
miracle &

meaning   what
found it let it

bless it burn it let them
turn into what

ever will be.

Two Descending a Staircase

after Marcel Duchamp and X. J. Kennedy

might just as well be one the way
his thumbs press deep into her flesh,
the way red stripes appear behind the nails
that scrape her back

as ground is raked to sprinkle seed.
It's in her interest to go slow.
Hurry the flesh? Her body leans
into his hands. The world

is bent on her bent neck and on
her skin goose bumps erupt. He rises too
and leans ahead, always a step or two

behind, and kind

of pushes her along.

Child and Woman

The moon is bigger than the girl is.
It rises as she bends, the woman.

The girl behind her.
And the moon rising
Immense and round
Filling up sight until knowing rests
Like a yellow dragonfly on a yellow leaf.
Until it flies the girl will not know it's there.

It is all the girl sees
For now, the enormity and then the whiteness of it
Before the others arrive strange

With laughter, to the bathhouse.

Cradle

Red poker pokes out beyond the blue
hydrangea where ashes were added
                    and the women,
eleven of them and every one
more than eighty,
move around in the erratic
              wobble of butterflies high on nectar;
                      the sunshine
has brought them out

into the garden where their heads sway
          over the flowerheads
like organs suspended off the spine,
seeming to float.   Things stayed in place back
when we were quadrupeds,
— spleen, intestines, colon, bladder, liver, stomach, pyloric
valve — swung heavily from the strong spine like a bridge
                  of ornaments.

    Now we are upright, now that the
slackened muscles no longer
cradle the liver, etc.
there is pouching and
sagging enough
to make each woman,   to all
but herself,
              unrecognizable.

Around the neck of one woman——
she's hung a photograph: Herself,
age 16:

       When they first met.

              It is they
who have brought each other here
as if each had gone
separately, and returned
after seventy years hauling multiple marriages and foreign travel and
if it makes me inextinguishably sad
— but they are not sad.

Notes on tact & the made up world

*My son Rudolf has more [tact] than I have, because he is my son,
and tact increases in every generation.* —Leopold Blaschka

Before he began making flowers, Leopold Blaschka sold glass eyes.

The glass flowers lodged under glass
make transparency's

virtue transparent, make perfection
the object of the object.

I sing   *glass for flesh   glass for cells.*
Flower that says something a flower can't.

Against the made-thing imagination scrapes its cheek,
for the beauty

is made poignant
for how out of unlikeliness the many stamened

Eucalyptus globula extends the gaze that studies it.

I touch   it it makes a sound.
I say it's singing.

Still why if I think it is plastic
will I like it less than if I think it is glass

which is the same thing
which is not the thing

itself. Once in a foreign city
I mistook for a line

of men pissing against a wall at night a line
of men praying against the wall.

The way
flowers don't break

makes me think
                        the less said.

And the backs of the men
performing their private devotions —

some wanting is containable.
I understand the wall

standing for nothing save
the attention of prayer and waste.

Old *Blaschka*,
where are those glass eyes

you made to order,
useless and convincing?

And now,
the blown fruit, whose promise was to render

visible, disease, for study, shows its allegiance to decay
in the dimming, pitting, flaking, in the crazing,

crizzle, and
it is moving

      in the display of parts
in the mimicry of stamen and pistil.

Nor does the mind imagining the parts
as parts and parts

as they might present themselves
in flower

attempt by this
to dissuade decay's sweet roughages.

How, then,

you are the one left.

You catch your breath.

How are you? friends ask.

Anymore
you're not yourself;
immense.

Everyone wants to touch it.
No everyone wants to just come close.

How are you? friends ask.

You don't catch it.

The painters told how massing the color
         leads the eye to some conclusion,
to an ending in sight.

What do you know, old friend, my vague gull?
What matters now? What's news?

Circling   back
to the moment your girl's mouth opened
                on impact—

        what do you hear?

Soft thuds like moths against the lit window
but oddly regular, like a small child's panting

walk up the hill after its rapid father.

Part of which is remembered and the other part is not forgotten

[Middle English, from Old French, from Latin musculus, *diminutive of* mus, *mouse]*

in the naming, as in the matter of
in the naming muscle.

The path was made of things cast off
too, and ground down
to be mute, indistinct.
Bark-browns sifted with cellulose and insect bits.

On top, plain sight, you were a thing
intact in miniature

of toenails, whiskers, naked tail   the color of birth.
Youna said *pink*   and I said *scrubbed.*
But you were even before scrubbed.

Slid onto the cardboard back
of a pad of paper, stiffest thing around,
you came alive.   Who was more startled?
How could skin the light sees through hold something in?
Soft without cushion,   soft in its surface, hard depths,

on my fingers the smell of what birthed you   the smell of your skin
the smell of inside of her.

      It presses itself.

Little bent knuckle,
you were tucked.